# Wikipedia Reader's Guide:

# Guide:

## The Missing Manual

D0555264

*John Broughton*

**Wikipedia Reader's Guide: The Missing Manual**
by John Broughton

Copyright © 2008 O'Reilly Media. All rights reserved.
Printed in Canada.

Published by O'Reilly Media, Inc., 1005 Gravenstein Highway North, Sebastopol, CA 95472

O'Reilly books may be purchased for educational, business, or sales promotional use. Online editions are also available for most titles (*http://safari.oreilly.com*). For more information, contact our corporate/institutional sales department: (800) 998-9938 or *corporate@oreilly.com*.

**Editors:**  Nan Barber and Keith McNamara
**Copy Editor:**  Sohaila Abdulali and Jill Steinberg
**Production Editor:**   Nellie McKesson
**Cover Designer:**   Karen Montgomery
**Illustrators:**   Robert Romano and Jessamyn Read

**Printing History:**
    April 2008:             First Edition

ISBN: 978-0-596-52174-5

[TM]

1208279314

# Contents

# Preface

## About the Author

 **John Broughton** has been a registered editor at Wikipedia since August 2005, with more than 15,000 edits by the time he wrote this book. His biggest Wikipedia endeavor has been the *Editor's index to Wikipedia* (just type that in the "search" box at the left of any Wikipedia page). This index lists every important reference page on Wikipedia, as well as hundreds of off-Wikipedia Web pages with useful information and tools for Wikipedia editors.

John's first experience with programming computers was in a 1969 National Science Foundation program. Since then, he's held various computer-related management positions in the headquarters of a U.S. Army Reserve division, worked in internal audit departments as a Certified Information Systems Auditor, and was the Campus Y2K Coordinator at U.C. Berkeley.

A Certified Management Accountant, John has a B.S. in Mathematical Sciences from Johns Hopkins University; an M.B.A. from Golden Gate University; an M.S. in Education from the University of Southern California; and a Masters in Public Policy from the University of California at Berkeley.

# Safari® Enabled

Safari offers a solution that's better than e-books. It's a virtual library that lets you easily search thousands of top tech books, cut and paste code samples, download chapters, and find quick answers when you need the most accurate, current information. Try it at *http://safari.oreilly.com*.

# Acknowledgements

The text in this booklet is largely adapted from the book *Wikipedia: The Missing Manual*, by John Broughton. Some text has been added by the author, with editorial guidance and other assistance from Keith McNamara, Alisson Walsh, and Nan Barber. Nellie McKesson was the production editor, and illustrations were done by Rob Romano. Keith Fahlgren provided DocBook support.

# CHAPTER 1

# Reader's Guide to Wikipedia

In mid-2007, a major survey found that more than a third of Americans regularly consulted Wikipedia. Since then, that percentage has probably grown, just as Wikipedia has—at the rate of several thousand new articles every day, plus the lengthening of articles via more than 100 edits every minute.

In January 2008, O'Reilly published *Wikipedia: The Missing Manual*. That book is a how-to manual for folks who want to edit Wikipedia articles and become more active in the Wikipedia community. This pocket guide is mostly about understanding and making the most of Wikipedia as a *reader*. But it also includes most of the first chapter of *Wikipedia: The Missing Manual*—Editing Your First Article—for when you're ready to consider the next step: contributing to the largest collective writing project in the world.

So, why do people contribute to Wikipedia? The question is relevant to you as a reader, because a writer's motivation offers some clues about the writing's trustworthiness. The reasons vary from person to person, and usually are a mixture of factors, but here are a couple:

- As a way of helping other people understand the world— and perhaps changing the world as a result.
- To give back to the community that provides a valuable resource by contributing to it.

- Clear, factual writing is challenging, interesting, and often fun. Working jointly with others on improving articles in Wikipedia is intrinsically rewarding.

## Some Basics

Wikipedia is a collaboratively written encyclopedia. It's a *wiki*, which means that the underlying software (in this case, a system called *MediaWiki*) tracks every change to every page. That change-tracking system makes it easy to remove (*revert*) inappropriate edits, and to identify repeat offenders who can be blocked from future editing.

Wikipedia is run by the not-for-profit *Wikimedia Foundation*; that's why you don't see advertising on any of its pages, or on any of Wikipedia's sister projects that the Foundation runs (more on those later). To date, almost all the money to run Wikipedia and its smaller sister projects has come from donations. Once a year or so, for about a month, you may see a fundraising banner instead of the standard small-print request for donations at the top of each page, but, so far, that's about as intrusive as the foundation's fundraising gets.

The Foundation has only about a dozen employees, including a couple of programmers. It buys hardware, designs and implements the core software, and pays for the network bandwidth that makes Wikipedia and its sister projects possible. But it doesn't have the resources to do any of the *writing* for those projects. All the writing (known in the community as *editing*) is done by people who get no money for their efforts, though plenty of personal satisfaction.

Wikipedia is an encyclopedia that anyone can edit. You don't have to register to edit articles. If you do register, you don't even have to provide an email address (although you should, in case you forget your password). Because of the variety and number of editors, Wikipedia is immense in scope—2.3 million articles as of April 2008, and over 1 billion words (more than 25 times as many as the next largest English-language encyclopedia, the Encyclopaedia Britannica). By the same token, Wikipedia is—and will continue to be—a work in progress.

# How Good is Wikipedia?

The best answer may be "Compared to what?" Wikipedia wouldn't be one of the world's top 10 most visited Web sites (that includes all 250-plus language versions, not just the English Wikipedia) if readers didn't find it better than available alternatives. To be sure, Wikipedia is an encyclopedia under construction. As the general disclaimer (see the Disclaimers link at the bottom of every page) says, "WIKIPEDIA MAKES NO GUARANTEE OF VALIDITY. Please be advised that nothing found here has necessarily been reviewed by people with the expertise required to provide you with complete, accurate or reliable information."

On the other hand, Wikipedia has been reviewed by a number of outside experts, most famously in an article published in *Nature* in December 2005. In that article, a group of experts compared 42 articles in Wikipedia to the corresponding articles in Encyclopaedia Britannica. Their conclusion: "The number of errors in a typical Wikipedia science article is not substantially more than in Encyclopaedia Britannica." (The actual count was 162 errors vs. 123.) That comparison is now more than 2 years old, and editors have continued to improve those 42 articles as well as all the others that were in the encyclopedia back then. (For a full list of outside reviews of Wikipedia, see the Wikipedia page *Wikipedia:External peer review*.)

None of which is to say that Wikipedia editors are wildly happy about the quality of many, if not most articles. Those most knowledgeable about Wikipedia have repeatedly talked about the need to improve quality, and that quality is now more important than quantity. The challenge is whether Wikipedia can implement a combination of technological and procedural changes that'll make a difference, because so far relatively

*Figure 1-1. Featured articles (articles with the highest assessed quality in Wikipedia) have a star in the upper right corner. You can click the star to learn how articles get their featured status.*

incremental changes haven't made much of a dent in the problem of accuracy.

So, should you trust Wikipedia? That should depend somewhat on the article. If you see a star in the upper right corner (see Figure 1-1), indicating a featured article, you can be virtually certain that what you'll read is correct, and that the cited sources back up what's in the article.

You'll find that each article contains clues to its reliability. If you see a well-written article with at least a reasonable number of footnotes, then you should be reasonably confident that almost all the information in the article is correct. If you see a lot of run-on sentences and templates noting a lack of sources, point of view problems, and so on, then you should be skeptical.

You can get more clues from the article talk (discussion) page; just click the "discussion" tab. At the top, see if a Wikipedia WikiProject (a group of editors working on articles of common interest) has rated the article. Also at the top, look for links to archived talk pages, indicating that a lot of editors have talked a lot about the article, and have therefore edited it a lot.

If there are no archive pages, and not much indication of activity on the talk page you're looking at, then the opposite is true—few editors have been interested in editing the article. That doesn't mean it's not good—some excellent editors toil in relative backwaters, producing gems without much discussion with other editors. Still, absence of editor activity should make you more doubtful that you've found an example of Wikipedia's best.

Bottom line: Think of Wikipedia as a starting place. If you're just interested in a quick overview of a topic, it may be an ending place as well. But Wikipedia's ideal is for articles to cite the sources from which their content was created, so that really interested readers can use those sources to get more information. If the editors at Wikipedia are doing things right, *those sources* are the ones that readers can absolutely depend upon to be informative and accurate.

# Navigating Within Wikipedia

There are two basic ways to find interesting articles in Wikipedia: Do a search, or browse, starting from the Main Page. Wikipedia has lots of organizing features depending on how you want to browse, like overviews, portals, lists, indexes, and categories. But for a bit of amusement, you can also try a couple of unusual ways to go from article to article, as discussed in this section.

## Searching Wikipedia

On the left side of each Wikipedia page, you'll find a box labeled "search", with two buttons—Go and Search. Wikipedia's search engine is widely acknowledged to be not particularly good. Your best bet to find what you want is to type the title you're looking for into the search box, and then click Go (or press Enter). If you're right, and Wikipedia finds an *exact* match, you'll be at that article. If it doesn't find an exact match, Wikipedia provides you with a link to "create this page", which you should ignore if you're searching only for reading purposes. It also provides you some search results. Figure 1-2 shows the result of a failed search for the title *Institute of Institutional Research*, including the start of some best guess results).

> Wikipedia is sustained by people like you. Please donate today.
>
> special page
>
> · Learn more abou
>
> # Search
>
> From Wikipedia, the free encyclopedia
>
> You searched for Institute for institutional Research [Index]
>
> For more information about searching Wikipedia, see Wikipedia:Searching.
>
> | Institute for Institutional Research | MediaWiki search ▾ | Se |
>
> **No page with that title exists.**
>
> You can create this page or request it.
>
> * See all pages within Wikipedia that link to this page.
> * See all pages that begin with this prefix.
>
> Results 1-20 of 36429
>
> 1 2 3 4 5 6 7 8 9 10 11 Next »
>
> * Burnham Institute for Medical Research

*Figure 1-2. When Wikipedia can't find an exact match to a Go request, it provides search results, but it also offers a link to create an article with the same name as the word or phrase you entered.*

---

**NOTE**

If you click "Search" for curiosity's sake, you'll just get some so-so search results. For example, if you search for *Reagan wife*, the article *Nancy Reagan* shows up 6th and *Jane Wyman* shows up 16th. Worse, the context Wikipedia's result page shows is terrible. With a Google search, by contrast, you can get these two names from the context shown for the first result without even having to click a link.

---

If you don't arrive at an article page when you click Go, and you don't find what you're looking for in the search results toward the bottom of the page, your next best move is to switch to another search engine. Wikipedia makes this very easy for you—just change "MediaWiki search" to another menu choice, as shown in Figure 1-3.

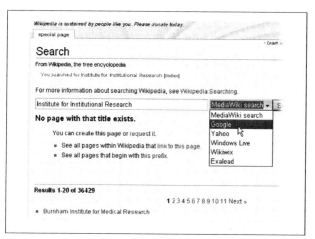

*Figure 1-3. Wikipedia makes it easy to pick another search engine. Here Google's being selected, but other search engines are available. Take advantage of this option if your initial Go attempt doesn't succeed.*

Figure 1-4 shows the search done again using Google. To those familiar with the Wikipedia search engine, it's not surprising that the top results are completely different.

---

### POWER USERS' CLINIC

## Searching from Outside Wikipedia

Figure 1-3 shows how to use an outside search engine to search Wikipedia, once your initial attempt to find an article has failed. You can do the same thing (get the same results as Figure 1-3, for example) without using a Wikipedia page initially, which may be easier.

To do so, type *site:en.wikipedia.org* into the search engine's search box, along with whatever word or phrase you were looking for. (The "en" prefix restricts results to the English Wikipedia, otherwise you could get

---

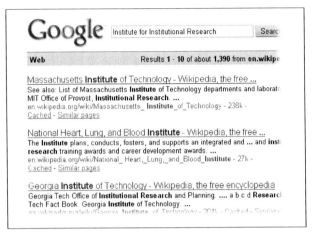

*Figure 1-4. The same search for "Institute for Institutional Research"
as in Figure 1-2, but this time searching with Google. The search
results are completely different.*

results from a version in the other 250 or so languages.)
This technique works for the big three: Google, Yahoo,
and MSN searches. If you use another search engine,
look at the "advanced search" option (often available
only after you do a search) for how to specify that the
results should come only from one domain.

You generally *don't* want to initiate an internal Wikipedia search via your browser. If you see a pull-down menu
that lets you pick Wikipedia as your search engine, ignore that choice. It just gets you to Wikipedia's internal
search engine, which, as discussed earlier, really isn't
very good.

The single exception to all the above is if what you're
searching has been added to Wikipedia in the last day
or two. If so, only the Wikipedia search engine is likely
to give you a successful search, because that engine is
the only one using the live database for its searches.

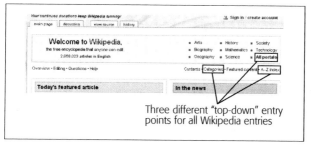

Three different "top-down" entry
points for all Wikipedia entries

*Figure 1-5. Wikipedia's Main Page is accessible via a single click from any other page in Wikipedia. At the top are three links to starting points within Wikipedia that provide different top-down views.*

> Everyone else has a not quite up-to-date *list* of Wikipedia pages, and not-quite up-to-date *versions* of Wikipedia pages.

## Navigating from the Main Page

You can also navigate Wikipedia via a number of different starting points. The best way to get to them is via the links near the top of the Main Page, as shown in Figure 1-5. Every Wikipedia page has a link to the Main Page, on the left side, in the navigation box below the Wikipedia globe. From the Main Page, you can see the vastness of Wikipedia via three different approaches: categories, portals, and the A-Z index.

### Categories

Any article may belong to one or more categories, which you'll find listed at the bottom of the article. Like everything else in an article, editors add the categories, so categories are only as accurate as the people who enter them; like everything else, if someone sees a mistake, she can fix it. When you click the Categories link shown in Figure 1-5, you'll see the master index (see Figure 1-6).

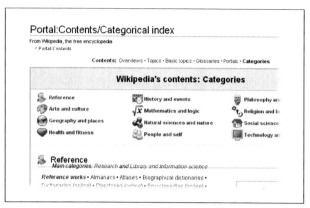

Portal:Contents/Categorical index

From Wikipedia, the free encyclopedia
‹ Portal:Contents

Contents: Overviews · Topics · Basic topics · Glossaries · Portals · **Categories**

**Wikipedia's contents: Categories**

| | | |
|---|---|---|
| Reference | History and events | Philosophy an |
| Arts and culture | Mathematics and logic | Religion and b |
| Geography and places | Natural sciences and nature | Social science |
| Health and fitness | People and self | Technology an |

Reference
*Main categories: Research and Library and information science*

*Reference works* · Almanacs · Atlases · Biographical dictionaries ·
Dictionaries (online) · Directories (online) · Encyclopedias (online) ·

*Figure 1-6. Here's the top-level list of categories. It's the starting point for drilling down to find all articles in any particular subcategory.*

The text in Figure 1-6 is hand-crafted, not computer-generated, but once you leave the page via a link on it, the lists you'll see will be computer-generated and thus completely current. For example, when you click Geography at the top of the index, that takes you to a section of the page called "Geography and places", with the main category Geography. Click that word, and you'll see Figure 1-7. If you're interested in Geography, you can drill down in whatever subcategory you want until you reach actual links to articles, and then follow them.

---

**NOTE**

Not every article in Wikipedia is intricately categorized. For example, at the bottom of the *Category:Geography* page, you see articles in that category which are *not* in any subcategory (you can't see them in Figure 1-7). Those may be truly unique articles, or articles just waiting for further categorization work.

---

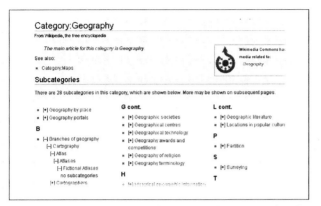

*Figure 1-7. The category* Geography *had 28 subcategories when this screenshot was taken. In the "B" section, you see an expansion of one of those subcategories, Branches of Geography, displaying all the sub-subcategories until there are no further ones, along one line of that subcategory.*

## Portals

From the Main Page, you can also follow the bolded link "All portals" to the main page for portals (Figure 1-8). Like categories, portals can be a great way to narrow down the number of articles you're particularly interested in reading, or to lead you to articles that you otherwise might never have known existed.

## The A-Z index

The third entry point link on the Main Page is the A-Z index. It's equivalent to browsing the shelves of a library, with the books in alphabetical order on the shelves. Figure 1-9 shows what you'll see if you click the "A-Z index" link at the top of the Main Page.

If you were trying, for example, to find the name of an article that began with an unusual pair of letters (say, *Cg*), then the A-Z index may be helpful (see Figure 1-10).

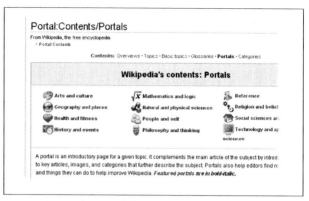

*Figure 1-8. Portals are probably one of the least known ways to find articles on Wikipedia. If you're particularly interested in a topic, one of the 500 or so existing portals can be a great page to bookmark.*

The alphabetical index to articles is actually more useful after you've drilled down one level. Now you have the option of searching for articles that start with three or four or even more characters.

### Other entry points

You may have noticed, in Figure 1-6 and Figure 1-8, a top-level row of links: Contents, Overviews, Academia, Topics, Basic Topics, and so on. Three of these (Overviews, Topics, Basic Topics) are also high-level entry points into Wikipedia that you might want to check out to see if one or more are interesting.

## Categories

Figure 1-5 showed you how to start a top-level organization of categories, by clicking the "Categories" link near the top of the Main Page.

---

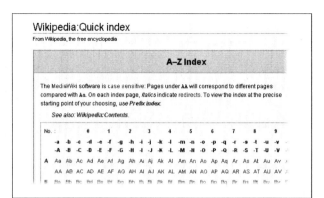

*Figure 1-9. The A-Z index (also called the Quick Index) lets you go directly to a list of articles beginning with any two characters: El or Na or Tr or whatever.*

## Other Ways of Navigating

When you're not on the Main Page, every Wikipedia page offers ways of browsing around. Most of them are in the list of links at the left.

### Random article

If you want to get a sense of the more than two million articles in the English language, a good way is to use the *Random article* feature. On any page on the *http://en.wikipedia.org* Web site, you find this link at upper-left (Figure 1-11) that you can click to ask the Wikipedia software to select one of those two million articles for you.

### What links here

When you're on an article page, you may find that another link on the left side of the screen, the first in the box labeled *toolbox* (see Figure 1-12) can also be fun to play with. Click *What links here*, and you're now looking at a list of incoming links to the article you were just reading.

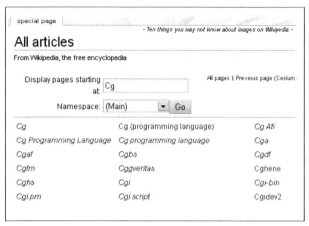

*Figure 1-10. If you pick a two-letter starting pair, in Figure 1-9, and click that link, here's what you see. The links in regular text are articles; the links in italics (the majority) are redirects, which take you to an article with a different name. Redirects are used for misspellings, for less common variants of a particular name, and for subjects that don't (yet) have their own articles, and are related to an existing article to which the reader will be directed.*

The list of links may seem random, but it's not—the oldest page (based on when the page was created) is listed first, the youngest page is listed last (and may very well not show on the screen, which normally lists just 50).

### Six degrees of Wikipedia

It can also be fun to just follow links from one article to another: For example, start at *Kevin Bacon*, then go to *Circle in the Square Theatre*, to *Theodore Mann*, to *Drama Desk Award*, to *New York Post*, and end up at *Alexander Hamilton*. You can also do the same with the "What links here" links mentioned in the previous section.

*Figure 1-11. On the left side of any Wikipedia page, the navigation box has a "Random article" link. Click again to go elsewhere. Click it 20 or 30 times, and you have a pretty good idea of Wikipedia's wide range of articles.*

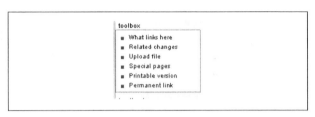

*Figure 1-12. The toolbox on the left of the screen includes a "What links here" link. Click it to see all the Wikipedia pages that link into the page you're on.*

## Wikipedia on the Go

Sooner or later, you're going to want to look something up on Wikipedia when you're not front of your laptop or desktop computer. Say you're touring Yellowstone National Park and want to find out about that geyser you're looking at. If you can get to the Web from your PDA or cell phone, then you can read Wikipedia just like any other Web site—that's a matter of course. But if your browser does a bad job of displaying Wikipedia articles, you have some options. And if you don't have mobile Web access, you can still use Wikipedia on the road by downloading what you want to read.

*Figure 1-13. The starting page of* en.wap.wikipedia.org *has a Go button but not a Search option. That makes it challenging to find an article if you're not sure of the exact name, and less than useful if you're just browsing.*

## Mobile Access

If your PDA or cell phone gives you Web access, it almost certainly has special Web browser software designed to fit large Web pages onto a small screen. But that browser is designed to make best guesses for the billions of pages on the Web, which means it doesn't understand the structure of Wikipedia pages.

If you want to read Wikipedia articles from a mobile device, the best thing to do is to go to a special web page as a starting point—a page that does understand how Wikipedia pages are set up—and go from there to the article you want. One such place is *http://en.wap.wikipedia.org*, an "official" Wikipedia site (see Figure 1-13).

The page Wikipedia:WAP access lists some other starting points from which you can also access mobile-tailored versions of Wikipedia articles. Here are two to consider:

- **wapedia.mobi**, which uses a separate (but current) database of Wikipedia articles. It has its own search engine, and (via the small "languages" link on the starting page) you can also read articles in virtually all other language versions of Wikipedia (see Figure 1-14).

---

**TIP**

Wapedia has a tailored version for Blackberries and other PDAs: start at *pda.wapedia.mobi/en/*.

---

- **wikipedia.7val.com** (see Figure 1-15) is perfectly suitable for reading Wikipedia, but was particularly designed for editing Wikipedia. (Unfortunately, as of this writing, editing of pages in the English language Wikipedia isn't possible through this site, due to open proxy issues.)

---

GEM IN THE ROUGH

## Let Your iPhone Suggest What Articles to Read

Many Wikipedia articles are geo-coded—they include coordinates for the longitude and latitude of the subject of the article. For example, the Golden Gate Bridge (according to Wikipedia) is at 37°49′11″N, 122°28′43″W. The application GeoPedia (for the iPhone only) uses information from Wikipedia and your location, as determined by the phone (using WiFi hotspot locations and cell-tower triangulation) to figure out what articles are relevant to where you are. It then lists those on your

---

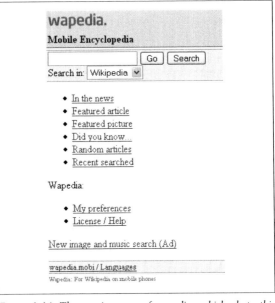

*Figure 1-14. The starting page of wapedia.mobi leads to this screen, when you click "English". (Tip: if you want the latest news, don't use Wikipedia; you'll see only relatively recent worldwide news important enough to require a major update of one or more Wikipedia articles.)*

iPhone screen for you to choose from. (Figure 1-16 shows an example of such a list.) As of this writing, the best information about the application is at *www.iphonefaq.org/archives/97405*; it's worth a search to see if you can find anything more recent, if you're interested.

Testers of this application have found problems installing it. Your mileage may vary, but the application isn't recommended at the moment. When it does work, GeoPedia may become a must-have application for iPhone owners.

*Figure 1-15. The starting page of wikipedia.7val.com features a link for logging in, something other services tailored for mobile access to Wikipedia do not have.*

## Wikipedia on a Mobile Hard Drive

Today's mobile devices, particularly those like the iPhone, have significantly large amounts of storage, which opens up another possibility for reading offline copies of Wikipedia articles of interest as the mood strikes you. The articles won't be the most recent versions, but they'll be accessible—without any charge for network access—whenever you want.

Wikipedia content is free for downloading, and anyone can sell that content and even add advertisements to it. So perhaps it's surprising that no one's yet offering Wikipedia articles in an easy-to-download form. Here are two options, both free, both with rough edges:

- If you have a Pocket PC or Pocket PC Phone running Windows Mobile 2003 Second Edition or Windows Mobile 5.0, or a Smartphone running Windows Mobile 5.0, you can store sets of Web pages (Web packs) on such a device using the mobile software developer Webaroo (*http://www.webaroo.com*). To do so, you download a Web pack to your notebook or desktop computer (Windows Vista, Windows XP, or Windows 2000) and then synchronize the download with the mobile device.

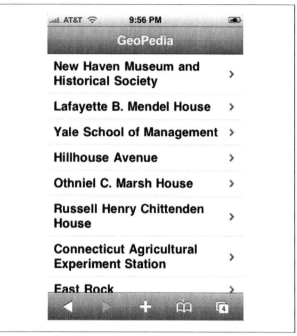

*Figure 1-16. A sample screenshot of GeoPedia in action. How useful it is depends critically on whether relevant articles in Wikipedia include (accurate) geographical coordinates, plus the accuracy of the iPhone's determination of where it is.*

It would be nice if Webaroo had a variety of web packs containing only Wikipedia articles—but it doesn't. There's just one Wikipedia-only Web pack—Webaroo calls it "The Wikipedia" (see Figure 1-17). Unfortunately, it's so large that it's not suitable for a mobile device, and there's no way to select pages from it (or other Web packs) to create a smaller Web pack. Worst, it's thoroughly out of date—the article on Barack Obama, for example, was from mid-2005.

*Figure 1-17. To download a Webaroo Web pack, you first have to download the Webaroo application. If you have 5 gigabytes or so of available storage on your laptop or desktop computer, you can download the English Wikipedia Web pack. If you have 1GB or more of RAM, you can then actually use that Web pack.*

- If you're an iPhone or iPod Touch owners, you might consider a very recently announced application called **wikipedia-iphone**. It includes all articles in Wikipedia as of October 2007. That takes up about 2GB of hard drive space, is a beta version, and the articles will, over time, become less and less current. If those limitations don't faze you, take a look (from your regular computer) at *http://collison.ie/wikipedia-iphone/* for details, including discussions about problems installing it.

# What Wikipedia is Not

To understand what Wikipedia *is*, you may find it very helpful to understand what Wikipedia is *not*. Wikipedia's goal is not, as some people think, to become the repository of all knowledge. It has always defined itself as an *encyclopedia*—a

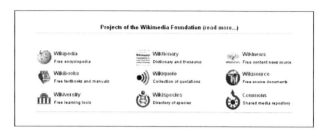

*Figure 1-18. The Wikimedia Foundation has eight parallel projects, the oldest of which is Wikipedia, plus the Commons, a central repository of pictures and other media.*

reference work with articles on all types of subjects, but not as a final destination, and not as something that encompasses every detail in the world. (The U.S. Library of Congress has roughly 30 million *books* in its collection, not to mention tens of millions of other items, compared to about two million *articles* in Wikipedia). Still, there's much confusion about Wikipedia's scope.

Wikipedia has a well-known policy (to experienced editors, at least) stating what kinds of information belong in the encyclopedia. The sister projects that the Wikimedia Foundation supports, such as Wiktionary, fulfill some of the roles that Wikipedia does not.

## Wikipedia's Sister Projects

The Wikimedia Foundation has seven projects that are parallel to Wikipedia, plus a project called the Commons, where pictures and other freely-usable media are stored for use by all projects in all languages (Figure 1-18).

*Two of the Foundation's sister projects overlap (or potentially overlap) with Wikipedia:*

- **Wiktionary** is a free, multilingual dictionary with definitions, etymologies, pronunciations, sample quotations, synonyms, antonyms and translations. It's the "lexical companion" to Wikipedia. It's common at Wikipedia to move (*transwiki*) articles to Wiktionary because they're essentially definitions.

- **Wikinews** and Wikipedia clearly overlap. A story in the national news (Hurricane Katrina, for example) is likely to show up on both. Unlike Wikipedia, Wikinews includes articles that are original writing, but the vast majority are sourced. Because of the overlap between the two, Wikinews has struggled to attract editors. Given a choice, most editors choose to work with Wikipedia articles, which are more widely viewed.

Three of the sister projects have a symbiotic relationship with Wikipedia:

- **Wikisource** is an archive of "free artistic and intellectual works created throughout history." Except for annotation and translation, these are essentially historical documents (fiction as well as nonfiction) that are in the public domain or whose copyright has expired.

- **Wikiquote** is a repository of quotations from prominent people, books, films, and so on. If you're reading a page of quotations by a person (like Mark Twain), you can jump to the Wikipedia article via a visible link and vice versa (see Figure 1-19). To date the English version has more than 15,000 pages.

- **Wikispecies** is a directory and central database of taxonomy, aimed at the needs of scientific users rather than general users. Much of its text is language-independent (Latin terms). In fact, it's the only Foundation project that doesn't have different versions in different languages. To date there are more than 125,000 articles.

The remaining two projects Wikipedia does not interact with, and these show the scope of the Foundation's goals:

- **Wikibooks** (previously called Wikimedia Free Textbook Project and Wikimedia-Textbooks), is for creating free content textbooks and manuals.

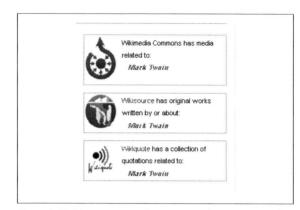

*Figure 1-19. It's easy to jump between Foundation projects when they have different types of materials about the same subject. Shown are three links in the "Mark Twain" article to the Wikimedia Commons (with pictures, as discussed on page xx), to Wikisource (all works published by Twain during his life are now in the public domain), and to Wikiquote.*

- **Wikiversity** is a place for the creation of learning activities and development of free learning materials. Its scope is wider than Wikibooks in that it includes things like course outlines and research and learning projects.

## Policy: What Wikipedia is Not

Wikipedia's policy, *What Wikipedia is Not*, is lengthy, so this section just hits the highlights. Aside from the guidelines that seem obvious to more experienced editors at Wikipedia ("Wikipedia is not a blog, Web space provider, social networking, or memorial site", "Wikipedia is not a mirror or a repository of links, images, or media files") and ones that follow from sister projects ("Wikipedia is not a dictionary", "Wikipedia is not a textbook"), here are several that readers and contributors frequently misunderstand:

- **Wikipedia is not a publisher of original thought**. You won't find ground-breaking analysis, original reporting, or anything else in Wikipedia that hasn't been published elsewhere first. (If you do find any of these, it's a violation of the rules and likely to be removed when other editors discover it.) Thousands of wikis do welcome original research and original writing, but Wikipedia isn't one of them. (You'll find hundreds listed at *http://WikiIndex.org*, a site not associated with Wikipedia.)

- **Wikipedia is not a directory**. Articles aren't intended to help you navigate a local bureaucracy, find the nearest Italian restaurant, or otherwise include information that other Web pages do a perfectly fine job of maintaining.

- **Wikipedia is not a manual or guidebook**. Wikipedia articles aren't intended to offer advice, or to include, tutorials, walk-throughs, instruction manuals, game guides, recipes, or travel or other guides.

  There actually are wikis for how-to stuff (*http://wikiHow.com*) and for travel (*http://Wikitravel.org*), but neither is affiliated with the Wikimedia Foundation and its projects.

- **Wikipedia is not an indiscriminate collection of information**. It's not the place for frequently asked question (FAQ) lists, collections of lyrics, long lists of statistics, routine news coverage, and "matters lacking encyclopedic substance, such as announcements, sports, gossip, and tabloid journalism."

# Wikipedia in Other Languages

If you go to the Wikipedia project's home page, *wikpedia.org* (as opposed to the English language Wikipedia site, *en.wikipedia.org*), you'll see a globe with a list of ten languages surrounding it—the ten language versions of Wikipedia with the largest number of articles. Scroll down, and you'll see more than 200 other languages. If you select something other than English, you'll be reading a completely different Wikipedia.

*Figure 1-20. The English Wikipedia article "Luberon" has links to five articles about that topic that appear in other language Wikipedias: German, French, Italian, Norwegian (nynorsk), and Occitan.*

---

**NOTE**

If you see ??? for one of the ten surrounding languages, that's Japanese. Your computer's set of fonts doesn't know how to display the characters.

---

It would be great if Wikipedia had a universal translator so an article created in or improved in one language Wikipedia would automatically appear in all the other language Wikipedias, but that's still a fantasy (at the moment). The reality is that editors of each Wikipedia generally use sources in their own language, which vary widely. Editors also focus their efforts on articles that most interest them and the readers of that language, which vary widely, and they spend relatively little time translating articles from one language Wikipedia to another.

There's another, more focused way to jump into another Wikipedia, useful if you happen to be able to read two or more languages. When you're looking at an article, you'll see, on the left side of the screen, a box labeled "languages". (You may need to scroll down to see it, and minor articles typically won't have the box at all.) There you'll find links to exactly the same topic in other language editions of Wikipedia. For example, Figure Figure 1-20 shows a box with five links for the article "Luberon," an area of three mountain ranges in France.

If you read French and wanted more information about Luberon, it's worth clicking the "Français" link—compare the table of contents in Figure 1-21.

# You Can Help

As mentioned earlier, Wikipedia calls itself "the free encyclopedia that anyone can edit". If you don't think that you personally have anything to add to it, you're wrong—Wikipedia is still far from complete. You—as a reader—can help when you see an article with a problem, or if you have suggestions for sources for improving an article, or if you search for an article and don't find it.

---

**TIP**

When you're thinking about fixing or adding to a Wikipedia article, make sure you have reliable sources at your fingertips first, as described on page 30, below.

---

## Articles with Problems

If you see vandalism in a Wikipedia article, it could easily have just happened, and an editor is in the process of fixing it. Wait 5 minutes or so, and then refresh your browser window (or leave the page and return). If it's still not gone, you can ask editors to help. Similarly, when you see something in an article that's incorrect or obviously missing (perhaps you had a question that you expected the article to answer), you can always ask about the problem, which makes it much more likely that active editors will fix it.

Asking about something in (or missing from) an article is an easy six-step process:

1. At the top of the article, you'll see a tab called "discussion". Click it.

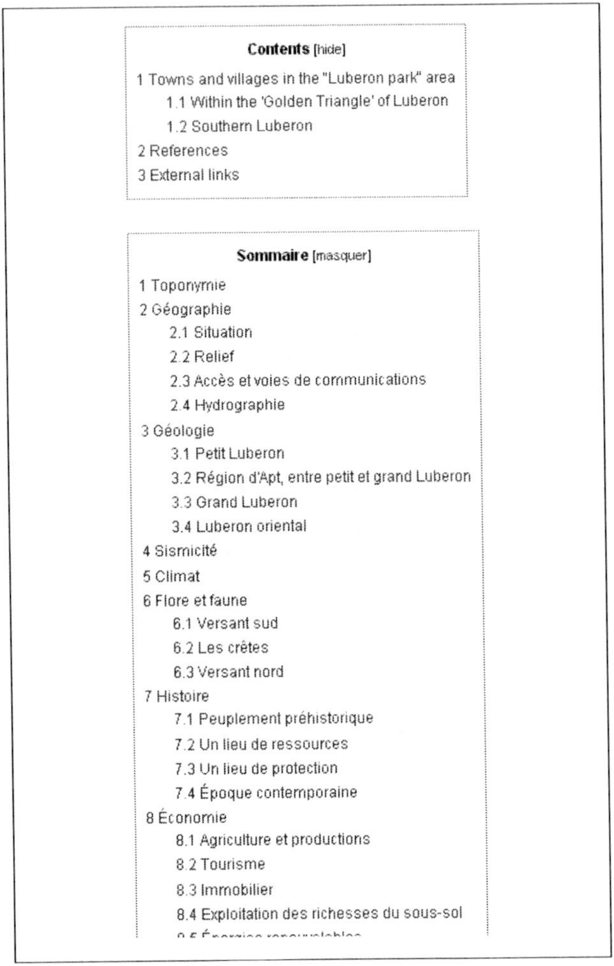

**Contents** [hide]

**Sommaire** [masquer]

*Figure 1-21. The article on "Luberon" in the English Wikipedia is much shorter than the article "Massif du Luberon" in the French Wikipedia; among other reasons, the latter is a Featured Article, the highest quality assessment possible in any Wikipedia.*

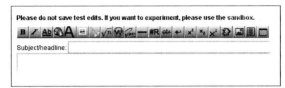

*Figure 1-22. Here's what the page should look like after step 3: It's ready for you to enter a brief summary ("Possible vandalism" or "Birthplace seems wrong" or whatever) and then, below the summary line, to type in your full comment or question.*

The article's talk (discussion) page opens.

2. Do a quick scan of the talk (discussion) page to see if your issue or question has already been asked.

   If so, you don't need to post anything; you're done.

   But if you're looking at something that looks like an error message, which starts, "Wikipedia does not have a talk page with this exact title. Before creating this page, please verify that an article called ... ", *don't worry*—this message means that your question couldn't possibly have been previously asked, because the talk page didn't even exist. You can go on to step 3.

3. Assuming your issue or question is new, click the "+" tab at the top of the talk page to start a new comment.

   You're in edit mode, with two boxes where you can type information.

4. Type a brief summary of the issue or question into the "Subject/headline" box at the top of the screen (Figure 1-22).

   Up to 10 words should be enough.

5. In the main edit box (see Figure 1-22 again), explain the issue/question. At the end of the last line of your comment, add a couple of spaces and then put four tildes next to each other (like this: ~~~~).

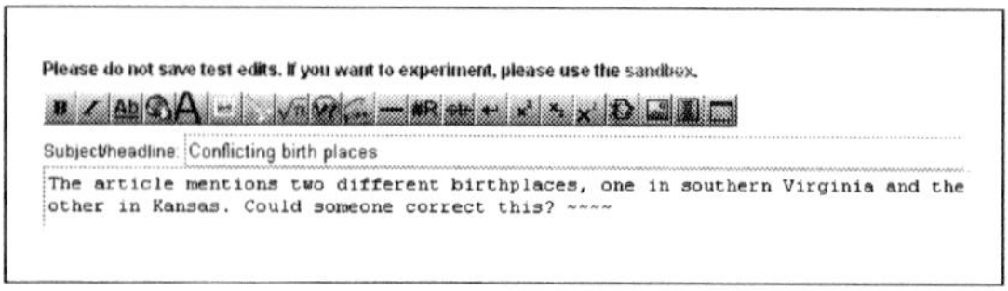

*Figure 1-23. Here's what the input screen shown in the previous figure looks like after someone has entered a section heading (summary) and a comment. It's now ready to be saved.*

The four tildes tell the Wikipedia software to put a signature and date-stamp there. Figure 1-23 shows an example of a comment after being typed in.

---

**NOTE**

The Wikipedia software records, in the page history, exactly the same information that displays when you add four tildes. So you're not revealing anything by "signing" your comment. If you don't, an automated editor (a *bot*) does it for you. You get more credit if you do the signing yourself.

---

6. Click the "Save page" button (you may have to tab down or scroll down or page down to see it).

   Voila! You've posted a comment to Wikipedia, thereby contributing to the improvement of an article (or bringing missed vandalism to the attention of other editors).

## Missing Information

Suppose you're reading an article or a section of a book about something interesting, decide to see if Wikipedia has more information, and find—to your surprise, perhaps—that the relevant Wikipedia article doesn't have the information that you were just reading, and doesn't mention the article or book that you have in hand. Clearly the Wikipedia article should cite that source, and should have that information—if it's interesting to you, it's interesting to other people. You can help Wikipedia

—and future readers—by leaving a note about the source. It's easy to do.

One quick caveat, first: Wikipedia wants only what it considers reliable sources—sources with a reputation for fact-checking and accuracy. That would include: major city newspapers in the United States, nonfiction books by major publishers, most magazines published nationally, and peer-reviewed articles in academic journals. But it would not include a high school newsletter or the self-published book by your next-door neighbor. This example assumes that what you're reading meets these criteria.

So, to help Wikipedia, leave a note on the talk/discussion page of the relevant article. Then, just follow the six steps in the previous section, but instead of leaving a question (step 5), leave a comment, saying something like "Here's a good source for additional information for the article." Then just type (or, if you're reading an article or book online, copy and paste) the following five things:

- The title of the article or book.
- The publisher (in the case of a magazine, just the name of the magazine).
- The date the article or book was published (if it's a book, that might just be the year, or the month and year).
- The name of the author(s). (Some newspaper articles don't list who wrote them; if so, skip this one.)
- The URL (Web address) of the book or article, if you're reading it online and other people can access it without a paid subscription or paying to download it. (If they do have to pay, but you can provide the URL where there is a free abstract or summary or initial paragraphs, that's a good substitute.)

Finally, as mentioned in step 5 on page 29, sign your comment with four tildes, and (step 6) save what you've posted. Soon thereafter, hopefully, you'll see other editors use your information to improve the article.

# Missing Articles

You've searched for an article and didn't find it, even using an outside search engine (page 5). Now what? Wikipedia has created a page where you can check to see if someone has already suggested that Wikipedia needs such an article. And that page, *Wikipedia:Requested articles*, has associated pages where you can add the name of the article as a suggestion if no one else already has.

Unfortunately, this page, and its associated pages, isn't particularly user-friendly for someone unfamiliar with Wikipedia editing. You have to pick the correct general topic area from a list of 10, then a topic area from what can be a long list, and then maybe even go down yet one more level just to see the area of a page where you're supposed to post.

Finally, when you're at the right area of the page, you have to figure out how to post your suggestion. If all the sections of all the associated pages were consistently formatted, you'd find instructions here on how to post to them—but they're not.

An easier way to suggest to the Wikipedia community that an article is needed is to find a relatively close *existing* article, and then, following the steps on page 27, post a note on the article's talk page. When you post, describe the topic that you looked for and couldn't find, and that you'd appreciate it if a more experienced editor added the subject at the *Wikipedia:Requested articles* page.

# CHAPTER 2

# Editing for the First Time

Anyone can edit Wikipedia—including you. That's right. There's no fee, and you don't have to register. You don't even have to have an email account (but if you're reading this book, you probably do). All Wikipedia articles are collaborative efforts, and you can jump right in and add your own knowledge with just a few clicks and some typing.

This chapter explains what you see when you look at an article in Wikipedia's editing window and how to practice, preview, and save your edits. You'll also learn a few more basic editing skills—how to create a link from one article to another, and how to edit a section of an article rather than the whole article. Once you've got these skills under your belt, you're ready for the first step in for-real Wikipedia editing: identifying an article in need of an edit.

---

**TIP**

You can dive right in and start editing without setting up a Wikipedia account (that is, getting a user name). However, there are advantages to having a user name— increased privacy and the ability to create new articles and a personal user page, to name two.

---

# The Wikipedia Way of Editing

Experienced Wikipedia editors understand one thing above all else: Wikipedia is a collaboration. There's no need to be intimidated, because you've got the support of an entire community of researchers, fact-checkers, and proofreaders. Keeping the following points in mind will get you into the right mindset for effective editing:

- **You don't need to know everything about Wikipedia to edit an article**. Wikipedia has literally hundreds of pages of policy, guidelines, and how-to information on topics such as capitalization, categorization, citations, copyrights, disclaimers, foreign language characters, headings, indentation, links, lists, neutrality, pronunciation, quotations, tags, and templates, to name just a few. *If you don't get something exactly right, don't worry—no one else gets everything right every time, either.*

- **You don't need to know everything about your subject to edit an article**. If you add something that's constructive and 90-percent right, that's far better than not doing an edit at all. As in sports, you don't need to hit a home run or score a goal on every play to be a valuable contributor. *If you don't get something exactly right, someone else is likely to come along and help by fixing or finishing it.*

- **You can contribute without editing at all**. If you see a problem in an article, but you don't (yet) know how to fix it, or you do know how to fix it, but you can't edit the article (some articles are fully protected, typically for short periods of time), you can still help by posting a constructive comment on the article's talk (discussion) page. *If you don't want to or can't edit an article directly, you can still help to improve it.*

# Practicing in the Sandbox

Even if you've done a lot of writing and editing with various types of software in the past, you'll need some practice with Wikipedia's tools. Fortunately, Wikipedia has a page called the *sandbox*, where editors can practice without worrying about damaging anything. In this chapter, you'll do your work in the sandbox, rather than editing actual articles.

Remember as you go through the book (or whenever you're editing), if you encounter a feature that you don't fully understand, you can always go to the sandbox and do some testing there. You won't break anything, and you can experiment as much as you want until you figure out exactly how things work. You can even practice duplicating the actual edits that are shown throughout this book.

From any page in Wikipedia, you can get to the sandbox in one of two ways:

- In the "search" box on the left side of the screen, type *WP:SAND*, and press Return. Make sure to type it with all capital letters and no space after the colon.

---

**TIP**

*WP:SAND* is a shortcut, and you'll see others like it throughout the book. If you feel you need to burn a few more calories, type in the search box the full name of the page you want to go to, in this case *Wikipedia:Sandbox*. Also note that Shift+Alt+F [Shift-Control-F on a Mac] will take you directly to the search box.

---

- Click the "edit this page" tab at the top of any page to go directly into edit mode. You'll see, toward the bottom of the screen (scroll down if necessary), "Your changes will be visible immediately." Immediately below, it says "For testing, please use the **sandbox** instead." The word "sandbox" is a bolded link—just click it.

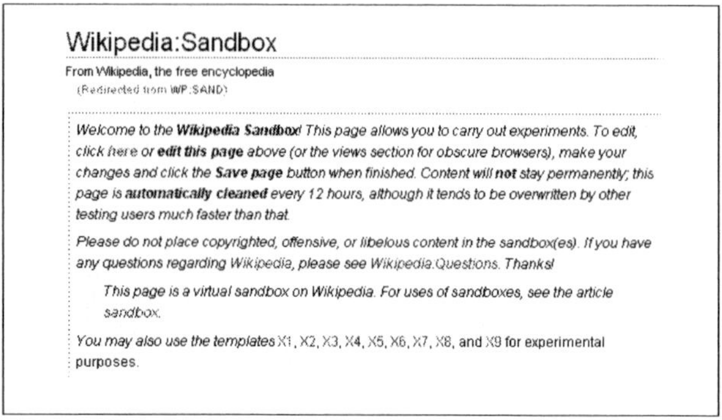

Wikipedia:Sandbox

From Wikipedia, the free encyclopedia
(Redirected from WP:SAND)

*Welcome to the **Wikipedia Sandbox**! This page allows you to carry out experiments. To edit, click here or **edit this page** above (or the views section for obscure browsers), make your changes and click the **Save page** button when finished. Content will **not** stay permanently; this page is **automatically cleaned** every 12 hours, although it tends to be overwritten by other testing users much faster than that.*

*Please do not place copyrighted, offensive, or libelous content in the sandbox(es). If you have any questions regarding Wikipedia, please see Wikipedia:Questions. Thanks!*

> *This page is a virtual sandbox on Wikipedia. For uses of sandboxes, see the article sandbox.*

*You may also use the templates X1, X2, X3, X4, X5, X6, X7, X8, and X9 for experimental purposes.*

*Figure 2-1. The top of the sandbox page, in normal mode. In normal mode, you can read what's on the screen, but not make any changes to it. To enter edit mode, just click the "edit this page" tab.*

Both ways get you to the sandbox quickly. Just use whichever method you find easier to remember. Figure 2-1 shows the sandbox before editing starts.

# Starting, Previewing, and Saving Your Edit

Editing in Wikipedia is much like using a very basic text editor, with a few word-processing tools thrown in. You type text into the edit box (less commonly written *editbox*), and then click buttons to preview and finally save your work.

## Adding Text

You edit Wikipedia articles in a big, white text box in the middle of the window. To get to that box, you must go into edit mode.

1. In the search box on the left side of the screen, type *WP:SAND*, and press Return to go to the sandbox.

   You'll do all your work in this chapter in the sandbox, so you won't actually change any Wikipedia articles.

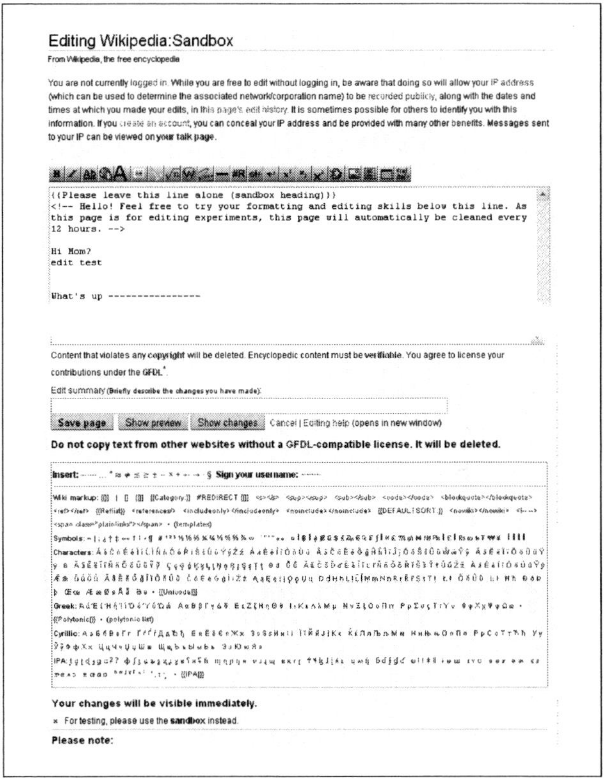

*Figure 2-2. The sandbox, in edit mode. The text in the box (the edit box) is only an example—what you see will depend on what the other editors have just done to the page. The edit toolbar along the top of the edit box is standard; it provides one-click options for the most common kinds of formatting of content. Also standard is all the text between the sentences "It will be deleted" and "Your changes will be visible immediately."*

2. From the sandbox page (Figure 2-1), click the "edit this page" tab.

   You're now in edit mode, complete with the edit box shown in Figure 2-2.

```
((Please leave this line alone (sandbox heading)))
<!-- Hello! Feel free to try your formatting and editing skills below this line. As
this page is for editing experiments, this page will automatically be cleaned every
12 hours. -->
```

*Figure 2-3. The edit box after deleting all but the top three lines. Now the edit box is ready for you to add text. Of what remains, the first line is a template (see page 49), and the second and third lines are an invisible comment—visible, that is, only when you're in edit mode.*

---

**NOTE**

If the bottom of Figure 2-2 looks intimidating, don't worry: There are only about two dozen items that editors actually use, except in exceedingly rare circumstances.

---

3. Delete everything but the first three lines, which are instructions.

   The edit box contents should look like Figure 2-3. In this box, you'll type some text that includes bold and italic formatting, and section headings.

   ---

   **NOTE**

   If someone else has deleted part or all of the top three instructional lines in Figure 2-3, don't worry—the steps on these pages will work just fine without them. But you may want to add them back to help others using the sandbox.

   ---

   If you compare Figure 2-1 to Figure 2-3, you may be puzzled about a couple things: What is the purpose of the curly brackets (the first line in the edit box in Figure 2-3), and why is the text in Figure 2-1 ("Welcome to the Wikipedia Sandbox! This page allows you to carry out experiments") not the same as the underlying text in Figure 2-3?

The answer to both questions is essentially the same: The curly brackets indicate a *template*, and the purpose of templates, generally, is to add standard text to a page. Because templates are so important—you'll find them everywhere at Wikipedia—there's a separate section on them later in this chapter (see page 49).

4. Type the text shown in Figure 2-4 (except the first three lines at the top, which should already be there) into the edit box.

   For this example, you don't have to type *all* the text if you don't want to. You can even type some text of your own invention, as long as it includes each of the following:

   - **Section headings**. Type two equal signs at the beginning and two more at the end of a line of text. (If you create at least four headings, Wikipedia automatically creates a table of contents, as you'll see in a moment.)
   - **Boldface**. Type three apostrophes (''') before and after the text you want to bold.
   - **Italic**. Type two apostrophes ('') before and after the text you want to italicize.

---

**NOTE**

Never put a blank space at the beginning of a line unless you want that line of text to stand out (which you never want in an article). With a blank space at the beginning, Wikipedia displays a line of text in a box with a light blue background. If it's a long line of text, the text goes off the screen to the right, requiring the reader to scroll to see it all.

---

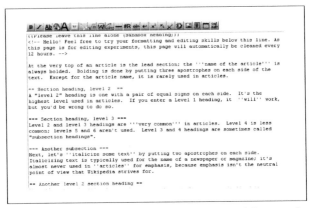

```
(!Please leave this line alone (sandbox heading))
<!-- Hello! Feel free to try your formatting and editing skills below this line. As
this page is for editing experiments, this page will automatically be cleaned every
12 hours. -->

At the very top of an article is the lead section; the '''name of the article''' is
always bolded.  Bolding is done by putting three apostrophes on each side of the
text.  Except for the article name, it is rarely used in articles.

== Section heading, level 2 ==
A "level 2" heading is one with a pair of equal signs on each side.  It's the
highest level used in articles.  If you enter a Level 1 heading, it  ''will'' work,
but you'd be wrong to do so.

=== Section heading, level 3 ===
Level 2 and level 3 headings are '''very common''' in articles.  Level 4 is less
common; levels 5 and 6 aren't used.  Level 3 and 4 headings are sometimes called
"subsection headings".

=== Another subsection ===
Next, let's ''italicize some text'' by putting two apostrophes on each side.
Italicizing text is typically used for the name of a newspaper or magazine; it's
almost never used in ''articles'' for emphasis, because emphasis isn't the neutral
point of view that Wikipedia strives for.

== Another level 2 section heading ==
```

*Figure 2-4. Typing this text into the edit box is a quick lesson in the three most common types of Wikipedia formatting. Putting equal signs on both sides of text turns it into a section heading (after you save your edit). Text surrounded by three apostrophes gets bolded; text surrounded by two apostrophes gets italicized.*

## Previewing

One of the most important things after doing an edit is to *preview* it—to see how it's going to look. For edits involving formatting, previewing is absolutely essential. But even if you've added only plain text, you should still preview it because you want to get in the habit previewing *every time*.

Experienced editors often skip previewing when making small, routine edits. Usually that's okay, but sometimes, to their embarrassment, after seeing what the page looks like after being saved, they realize they need to do another edit to fix their own mistakes. So, until you've become an experienced editor, preview your work every time.

Before you click the "Show preview" button, however, you should do one more thing—provide a summary of the edit you just made. You should do this *now*, rather than later, because previewing will also show you what the edit summary will look like. Think of the edit summary as a way for you to explain

*Figure 2-5. When you add an edit summary, make it descriptive but concise. (As noted in Figure 2-2, the checkboxes for "This is a minor edit" and "Watch this page" are visible only if you're a registered user who is logged in.)*

your edit to other editors. The explanation can be very brief ("typo," "revert vandalism") or it can be lengthy (up to 200 characters). Keep it as short as you can, and make it as long as you need to.

1. In the "Edit summary" box (Figure 2-5), type a few words to describe the purpose of your edit.

   In other words, follow the instructions in fine print: "Briefly describe the changes you have made." For example, in this case you might type *Test edit – first time using the Sandbox*. (See the box below for information about edit summaries.)

   Once you've added an edit summary, it's time to check your work.

---

## In Summary

Filling in the "Edit summary" box, to explain your edit, takes only a few seconds but can save other editors lots of time. These summaries show up on each article's "history" tab, on the page that lists a given editor's contributions, and pretty much everywhere else that a list of edits appears within Wikipedia: They're important.

Edit summaries should be meaningful to all editors. If you encounter an abbreviation or other text you don't

---

understand, check the page *Wikipedia:Edit summary legend* (shortcut: *WP:ESL*), which has a pretty comprehensive list.

Here are some common edit summaries:

- "Copyediting"
- "Removed duplicate text in section"
- "Splitting section in two with subheadings, adding new information and sources"
- "Added material, changed section heading"

If you start editing articles regularly, here's another advantage to creating your own Wikipedia account: Once you've created an account, you can change a setting so that you get a reminder to add an edit summary, if you've forgotten one. When logged in, click the My Preferences link (in the upper-right area of the screen), then click the "editing" tab, and at the bottom of the list of options, turn on the "Prompt me when entering a blank edit summary" checkbox. Click Save. Once you've done that, you'll never have to worry about inadvertently forgetting to fill in the "Edit summary" field.

2. Click the "Show preview" button just below the edit window (the button is shown in Figure 2-5) to see what the Wikipedia page will look like after you save your edit.

   A Wikipedia preview screen has three parts. The very top of the screen (Figure 2-6) shows a warning that you're not looking at a saved version of the page. The middle and bottom of the screen (Figure 2-7) show both what the page will look like after you save it (if you don't change it further) and the edit box and related tools.

3. Now's your chance to fix mistakes before anyone else can see them. Just make any changes you want in the edit box, and click "Show preview" again.

*Figure 2-6. At the very top of the preview screen there's always a warning, in red, that you're looking at a preview, not something that has been saved.*

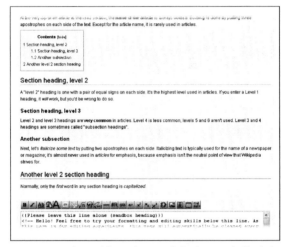

*Figure 2-7. The middle and part of the bottom half of the preview screen, showing how the edit from Figure 2-4 looks after saving the page. Wikipedia automatically adds a table of contents for articles that have four or more section headings. At bottom is the now-familiar edit box, so you can make corrections or improvements to your article.*

When you're satisfied with what the preview shows, it's time to save the edit, which will change the version that readers see when they come to the page.

**Edit conflict: Wikipedia:Sandbox**

From Wikipedia, the free encyclopedia

Someone else has changed this page since you started editing it, resulting in an edit conflict. The upper text area contains the page text as it currently exists (without your changes). Your version of the page (with your changes) is shown in the lower text area. You will have to merge your changes into the existing text in the upper text area to incorporate your edits. Only the text in the upper text area will be saved when you press "Save page", all other changes in the lower text area will be lost.

You are not currently logged in. While you are free to edit without logging in, be aware that doing so will allow your IP address (which can be used to determine the associated network/corporation name) to be recorded publicly, along with the dates and times at which you made your edits, in this page's edit history. It is sometimes possible for others to identify you with this information. If you create an account, you can conceal your IP address and be provided with many other benefits. Messages sent to your IP can be viewed on your talk page.

*Figure 2-8. The top of a page when there's an edit conflict. If you're logged in, you see only the top paragraph of information.*

## Saving

Click the "Save page" button (see Figure 2-5 for the location of this button, if you need to). At this point, one of three things happens:

- Most of the time, the page changes, incorporating your edit. That is, the page looks like what it did when you looked at it in preview mode, except now there is no preview warning on top. Your edit is complete; you're done.

- You might see a *cached* version of the page. You'll see a version of the page that looks like it did before you edited the page. In this case, you should refresh the page in your Web browser; typing Ctrl-R (⌘-R on the Mac) does the trick in most browsers. Once you see your edit has taken affect, you're done. (In the rare case where refreshing the page doesn't work, you need to tell your computer to remove old copies of *everything*. See the page *Wikipedia:Purge*; shortcut *WP:PURGE*.)

- The worst case scenario is that Wikipedia refuses to make the change because someone else changed the page while you were editing it. Figure 2-8 shows what the page will look like in case of an *edit conflict*.

# Wiki Markup: From Edit Box to Screen

Earlier in this chapter, you learned how to create section headers, and to format text as bold or italic (see Figure 2-4). Such formatting is called *wiki markup*. As you continue through this book, you'll learn about every type of markup you're likely to encounter. As a new editor, though, you need to learn three things right away: to recognize the types of markup, how templates are used, and how to create links between articles.

## Types of Markup

Besides headings, bold, and italic text, you'll encounter the following types of markup as you edit articles:

- **{{pagename}} or {{pagename | info1 | info2 }} or {{pagename | this= info 1 | that= info2}}**.The double curly brackets indicate a template. An example of a template appeared in Figure 2-3 and was discussed immediately thereafter. Templates are discussed in more detail later in this chapter (page 49).

- **[[Article name]] or [[Article name | other name]]**. Double square brackets create internal links (wikilinks), which are hyperlinks between pages in Wikipedia.

- **[http:url] or [http:url some text]**. Single square brackets around a URL create external links. This formatting is discussed in *Wikipedia: The Missing Manual*.

- **<ref> text possibly with a URL </ref>** and **<references />**. These are footnote tags—the text between the tags is the footnote itself—plus the instruction to Wikipedia as to where to display the footnotes. Footnotes are also described in detail in *Wikipedia: The Missing Manual*.

- **<blockquote> text </blockquote>** and **<math> numbers and symbols</math>**. In articles, you'll find a few other types of paired tags besides the *<ref>* tags for footnotes; blockquote and math tags are among the more common. Tags normally come in pairs, and the ending tag *must* have a slash character ("/") as its second character if it is to work properly.

---

**TIP**

One exception to the rule of pairs is the *<br>* tag that inserts a new line (for example, in a template). It's just the single <br> tag with no closing tag. If you type *<br/>* or *</br>*, that does the same thing as *<br>*. (The "br" stands for "break," as in "line break.")

---

- **<!-- Your comment text goes here -->**. This markup turns the text inside into an invisible comment; an example appears in Figure 2-3. "Invisible" means that the text doesn't display in normal viewing mode; you can see it only in edit mode.
- **{| bunch of stuff with lots of vertical lines |}**. This formatting creates a table. You can learn more about creating tables in Chapter 14 of *Wikipedia: The Missing Manual*.
- **One or more rows starting with an "*" or a "#"**. These characters create lists within an article (the "#" numbers the list, while the "*" just puts a bullet at the beginning of a line).
- **[[Category:Name]]**. This markup looks like a wikilink, and it is, in a way, but it puts a category link at the bottom of a page.

## How to Create Internal Links

Linking one article to another is very easy—with good reason. Links to other articles can add a lot of value to an article because readers can follow the links whenever they come across a word they don't know a lot about. Good places to add internal links include the lead sections of articles and at the beginning of new sections within articles. A reader should always be able to get to important, related articles via a link.

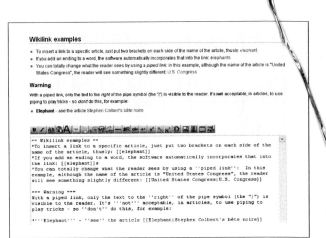

**Wikilink examples**

- To insert a link to a specific article, just put two brackets on each side of the name of the article, thusly: elephant
- If you add an ending to a word, the software automatically incorporates that into the link: elephants
- You can totally change what the reader sees by using a *piped link*; in this example, although the name of the article is "United States Congress", the reader will see something slightly different: U.S. Congress

**Warning**

With a piped link, only the text to the *right* of the pipe symbol (the "|") is visible to the reader. It's **not** acceptable, in articles, to use piping to play tricks - so *don't* do this, for example:

- **Elephant** - *see* the article Stephen Colbert's bête noire

```
== Wikilink examples ==
*To insert a link to a specific article, just put two brackets on each side of the
name of the article, thusly: [[elephant]]
*If you add an ending to a word, the software automatically incorporates that into
the link: [[elephant]]s
*You can totally change what the reader sees by using a ''piped link'': In this
example, although the name of the article is "United States Congress", the reader
will see something slightly different: [[United States Congress|U.S. Congress]]

=== Warning ===
With a piped link, only the text to the ''right'' of the pipe symbol (the "|") is
visible to the reader. It's '''not''' acceptable, in articles, to use piping to
play tricks - so ''don't'' do this, for example:

*'''Elephant''' - ''see'' the article [[Elephant|Stephen Colbert's bête noire]]
```

*Figure 2-9. Compare what's been typed into the edit box (bottom) to what's in the preview portion of the page (top).*

In the edit box, just place paired square brackets around the name of the article you want to link to, for example: *[[Winston Churchill]]*. Figure 2-9 shows the sandbox again, in preview mode with some internal links sprinkled in.

Another kind of internal link—a piped link—is extremely useful for situations where naming varies by country. For example, you've typed the following sentence in your article: "San Francisco has an extensive public transportation system," and you want to link the words "public transportation" to the relevant article. Trouble is, there's no article in Wikipedia named "public transportation." There is, however, an article named "public transport," which was probably written by someone who speaks British English. You don't care what it's called, you just want your readers to be able to go to that article. Here's how to create the link while having the article read "public transportation": *San Francisco has an extensive [[public transport|public transportation]] system.*

# To Link or Not to Link

Wikilinks make writing on a wiki much easier than writing on paper, because you don't have to explain jargon (just link to the relevant article), and you can provide a smidgen of contextual information on people, places, and things by linking to separate articles. The resulting wiki page is easier for more people to read, since advanced readers don't have to skip explanations they don't need, and the less advanced readers can follow links as necessary to get more context.

As helpful as links are, it's counterproductive to create internal links for a large percentage of words or phrases in an article—Wikipedians call that *overlinking*. You don't want your readers to spend more time hopping around to other articles than reading the one they came for.

To help decide whether you need to insert a link into an article, think of a link as a cross-reference in a book: "*see* such-and-such." If you wouldn't ask readers to turn to another page to read about something, don't provide a link for it either. Here's a case of excessive cross-referencing:

Mahatma Gandhi was a major (*see* "major") political (*see* "political") and spiritual (*see* "spiritual") leader (*see* "leader") of India (*see* "India") and the Indian independence movement (*see* "Indian independence movement").

Here are some general guidelines:

- Don't link plain English words or phrases; do link technical terms.
- Don't link the same word or phrase multiple times, at least not in the same section of an article.

- Avoid linking two words that are next to each other, because these will look to the reader as if they are a single link (if necessary, reword the sentence).

## Understanding and Using Templates

As mentioned on page 39, if you go into edit mode and see some text surrounded by two curly brackets, like this: *{{page-name}}*, you're looking at a template. A template tells the software to get text and formatting instructions from another place and insert that formatted text into the article when the article is displayed.

Here's a common example: If you see the *{{fact}}* template in the edit box when you're editing an article, it's telling the software to go to the page *[[Template:Fact]]*, get the text there (including formatting), and insert that text into the article when the article is displayed for readers. The *{{fact}}* template, displays the following text: *[citation needed]*.

Templates are widespread for a number of reasons:

- **Consistency**. Every cleanup template looks the same, each type of infobox looks the same, and so on. Editors don't have to constantly figure out how to present a particular type of information in an article.

- **Time savings**. You don't have to type out standard information, and you don't have to know how to format information in standard ways (such as superscript or message boxes). You just have to find out the name of the template and put it in double curly brackets. The software does the rest.

- **Automatic updating**. If the Wikipedia community decides to change a template, changing just one page—the template page itself—automatically changes what's displayed on every other page that uses the template. (High-use templates are protected from being changed by normal editors, to prevent easily-done extensive vandalism.)

- **Categorization**. Templates can include text that puts a page into a category. Then you and other editors can go to the category page to find, for example, all articles that have been categorized as needing copyediting.

For more details on using templates, see *Wikipedia: The Missing Manual*.

# Editing Article Sections

Inexperienced editors often work on *entire* articles in edit mode even though they're making changes only to *one section* of that article. Not only does this make it more difficult for other editors to understand what an editor did, but it also significantly increases the chances of an edit conflict. So, an important rule of editing is: *Don't edit an entire page if you're changing only one section of the page*.

## Editing One Section

You'll know an article has sections if you see a table of contents near the top of the article. Even if there is no table of contents, if you see headings within an article, then the article has sections that can be edited. Figure 2-10 shows an article with no table of contents but with three headings that indicate sections that can be edited.

If you click one of the three "edit" links in Figure 2-10, then the edit box shows *only* the text in the section, not the text of the entire article. That makes it easier to edit (less text in the edit box), and it significantly lessens the likelihood of an edit conflict, because if another editor is editing a different section, your two edits can't collide.

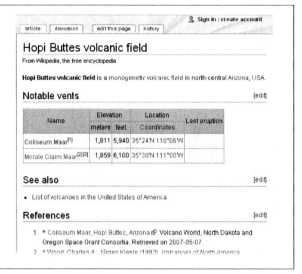

Figure 2-10. An article with three sections that can be separately edited. To edit a specific section, click an "edit" link on the right side of the page.

---

**TIP**

Sometimes editing an entire article at once is necessary —for example, if you're moving sections around, or moving text from one section to another. But often when you plan to edit two or three sections of an article, you can efficiently do these as separate edits of individual sections, rather than editing the entire article. If nothing else, it makes previewing much easier (but the preview shows only *part* of the article, not the entire article).

---

# Editing the Lead Section

From the previous section, you know the importance of editing *only* a section rather than an entire article, whenever possible. But you may have noticed that in Figure 2-10 there was no

[edit] link for the first sentence in the article, what Wikipedia calls the *lead section*. So, it appears that if you want to edit that section, you have to click the "edit this page" tab, just as if you wanted to edit the entire article.

In fact, it *is* possible to edit only the lead section of an article, though most editors don't know how. There are actually three different options:

- The manual way is to click the [edit] link for a section below the lead section, then go to the URL at the top of the screen and change the number at the end of the URL to "0". (The lead section of an article is always numbered section "0".) Press Enter, and you're then editing the lead section.

- The most complicated way is to add JavaScript code to your personal JavaScript page, to give you either a special tab (the "0" tab) or an "edit" link. You can find these scripts in the "Navigating to Edit page" section of the page *Wikipedia:WikiProject User scripts/Scripts* (shortcut: *WP:JS*). (Note: To do so, you must be a registered editor.)

- The easiest way is to click the "my preferences" link on the upper right of the page (which you won't see unless you have a registered account and are logged in), go to the "Gadgets" tab. Select "Add an [edit] link for the introduction section of a page", and then click the Save button. Thereafter, whenever you're editing an article, you'll see something similar to Figure 2-11.

## Editing for Real

Now that you've read about the basics of editing, and (hopefully) followed the step-by-step instructions for doing a sandbox edit, you're almost ready to start editing actual articles. Before you do so, you need to understand a bit more about the rules of Wikipedia. Then you'll be prepared to find some articles that you can improve.

Figure 2-11. After you've selected the option to add an edit link for the lead section on the Gadgets tab of the "My preferences" page, you see a new edit link to the right of the title of every article. Clicking that link will open the top section of the article for editing. (If you don't see such a link, make sure you bypassed your browser's cache as described at the bottom of the Gadgets tab.)

## Wordsmithing Versus Adding Information

Taken to an extreme, there are basically two kinds of edits (other than removing vandalism, spam, and other problematic material):

- You can change the wording and/or formatting of an article, leaving the information in the article more or less intact.
- You can add new information.

It's worthwhile to do a bit of research about correct documenting of sources in Wikipedia articles before you start adding new information, but if you want to jump right into wordsmithing, read on.

## A Few Words about Content

Wikipedia has three core policies for content. Two of them, *no original research* and *verifiability*, can be overlooked for the moment (though you can read about them in detail in *Wikipedia: The Missing Manual*). The third, *neutral point of view*, is worth mentioning now, because wordsmithing is often about a point of view.

Consider, for a moment, the goal of the people doing public relations or in a marketing department: to write about organizations, products and services, and leaders in a way that casts them in the best possible light. Or consider the wording of a press release by a political party, which tries to make the opposition look as bad as possible. In both of these situations, the writers have what Wikipedians call an extreme point of view (POV). By contrast, Wikipedia's policies require editors to follow these principles:

- Present significant viewpoints in **proportion** to the (published) prominence of each. Fringe theories, for example, deserve much less space (word count) in an article than mainstream/conventional theories.

- **Represent fairly** any differing views about a topic. *Fairly* means presenting the best case for each view, while avoiding extreme rhetoric from either side.

- Write **without bias**. The best way to do this is to write about facts, not about opinions. For example, instead of saying "X murdered Y," which is an opinion (was it self defense?), write "X was convicted of murdering Y," a documentable fact.

Wikipedia has much, much more detail that you can read about this policy (type the shortcut *WP:NPOV* in the search box on the left of the screen). Many (probably most, maybe even all) editors at Wikipedia have very strong opinions about one thing or another—cultural values, religion, politics, science, whatever. Good editors avoid problems by either focusing on making articles as factual as possible or working on articles where their potential biases aren't triggered. So if you're absolutely, positively sure you're right about a topic where many, and possibly most, other editors at Wikipedia wouldn't agree with you, it's a good idea to work on the other two million (or so) articles in Wikipedia that *aren't* about that topic. (Keep in mind that there are lots of places on the Web —blogs, personal pages, wikis other than Wikipedia, and more —where proactive opinions *are* welcome.)

navigation

* Main page
* Contents
* Featured content
* Current events
* Random article

*Figure 2-12. The "Random article" link. Click this to go to one of the about two million articles in Wikipedia.*

## Selecting a Random Page

Ready to edit? If so, you'll want to find articles that you can improve with copyediting. One way is to click the "Random article" link on the left side of the screen (see Figure 2-12).

When you click this link, there's a good chance you'll get a very short article (a *stub*), or a list, or a page that starts "XYZ may refer to ..." followed by a list of related topics (a *disambiguation* page), or a very specialized article. You can edit these, of course, but you may want to try again. When you get an article that you're not interested in editing, just click the "Random article" link again. (Do this twenty or so times, and you get a reasonable sense of the variety in the almost two million articles in Wikipedia.)

## Working on a Known Problem

An alternative to using the "Random article" link is to go to articles that other editors have identified as problematic. Several good places to find such articles are:

* Wikipedia:Pages needing attention (shortcut: *WP:PNA*)
* Wikipedia:Requests for expansion (shortcut: *WP:RFE*)
* Category:Wikipedia articles in need of updating (shortcut: *CAT:UP*)

- Category: Wikipedia maintenance (shortcut: *CAT:M*)

When you see the name of an article that seems interesting, just click the article name to go to it and start editing as described earlier in this chapter.

---

**WORD TO THE WISE**

## Spelling Doesn't (Always) Count

If you find what looks like a spelling mistake, don't leap into edit mode and correct it. What you think is an error may be a perfectly legitimate spelling in context. For example, you may have stumbled upon a national variant of a word: What is "analyse" in the United Kingdom is "analyze" in the United States; neither is wrong.

Wikipedia's spelling rules are mostly based on consistency. For example, don't mix variants of the same word within a single article. If an article is about (say) a major city in Australia, then spellings used in that country are correct for the article; if an article has evolved primarily with one variety of English, the whole article should conform to that variety. (For more details, use these shortcuts to get to two guideline pages: *WP:SPELLING* and *WP:ENGVAR*.)

---